A Guide to Generative AI Design with Stable

Diffusion, DALL-E 2

Contents

Part 1: Diving into Generative AI Design

This section will equip you with the foundational

knowledge of generative AI design. We'll break down

the core concepts, explore how machine learning

fuels this creative process, and delve into popular

techniques like Generative Adversarial Networks

(GANs) and Diffusion Models.

Chapter 1: Unveiling the Power of Generative AI

Imagine a tool that can take your textual descriptions and turn them into vibrant images. That's the magic of generative AI design! But how does it work? Let's break it down:

- **Demystifying Generative AI Concepts:** Generative AI refers to a subfield of artificial intelligence focused on creating new content, in this case, visual content. It leverages machine learning algorithms trained on massive datasets of images and text to learn patterns and relationships. This allows the AI to generate entirely new images that resemble the data it has been trained on.

- **How Machine Learning Fuels Image Creation:** Machine learning algorithms are like students constantly learning from vast amounts of data. In generative AI design, the algorithm analyzes existing images and text descriptions, identifying underlying patterns and connections. This knowledge empowers it to "imagine" and create new images that adhere to those patterns.

- **Exploring Different Generative AI Techniques:** There are several techniques used in generative AI design, each with its strengths and weaknesses. Here are two prominent ones:

  - **Generative Adversarial Networks (GANs):** Imagine two AI models locked in a competition. One, the generator, tries to create realistic images, while the other,

the discriminator, tries to determine if an

image is real or AI-generated. This

constant battle refines both models,

resulting in the generator producing

increasingly realistic images.

- **Diffusion Models:** This approach starts

  with a noisy image and progressively

  removes the noise, step-by-step, until a

  clear image emerges. The AI learns the

  process of "denoising" by analyzing real

  image datasets, allowing it to eventually

  create entirely new images from scratch.

Chapter 2: Meeting the AI Design Powerhouses

Now that you understand the core concepts, let's meet some of the leading generative AI design tools:

- **Stable Diffusion:**This open-source powerhouse offers incredible creative freedom. You can provide detailed text descriptions and generate stunning images.

- **DALL-E 2:**Developed by OpenAI, DALL-E 2 is known for its exceptional image quality and ability to generate variations on a concept.

- **Exploring Additional Options:** The world of generative AI design is constantly evolving.

Beyond Stable Diffusion and DALL-E 2, there are numerous tools emerging, each with its unique strengths. We'll explore some of these options in the next section.

Part 2: Mastering the Art of the Prompt

The prompt is your bridge to the world of generative AI design. It's the set of instructions you give the AI to translate your vision into an image. Mastering the art of crafting prompts unlocks the full potential of these tools.

Chapter 3: Crafting Compelling Prompts: The Key to AI Design Success

Think of a prompt as a detailed recipe for the AI. The more specific and clear you are, the better the results will be. Here's what you need to know:

- **The Art of Effective Prompt Writing:**
  - **Clarity is King:** Use concise and unambiguous language. Avoid vague terms like "beautiful" or "interesting." Instead, use specifics like "vibrant colors" or "art deco style."
  - **Details Matter:** The more details you provide, the more refined the output will be. Describe objects, their placement,

lighting, and even emotions you want conveyed.

- **Leveraging Textual Prompts and Image Inspiration:**

  - **The Power of Words:** Textual descriptions are the foundation of your prompt. Use descriptive language that paints a vivid picture for the AI.

  - **Visual Inspiration:** Sometimes, a picture is worth a thousand words. Include reference images alongside your text prompt. This helps the AI understand the style and aesthetics you're aiming for.

- **Advanced Prompt Engineering Techniques for Fine-Tuning Results:**

- **Negative Prompting:** Want to steer the AI away from certain elements? Use negative prompts! For example, "A photorealistic portrait of a woman, not a cartoon" tells the AI what you don't want.

- **Style Transfer:** Want your image to mimic a specific artistic style? Include references to paintings, artists, or even historical periods in your prompt.

Case Study: Creating a Book Cover with DALL-E 2

Imagine you're designing a cover for a fantasy novel. Here's a basic prompt: "A powerful wizard casting a spell in a dark forest."

This might generate an okay image, but with some prompt engineering, we can elevate it:

- **Improved Prompt:** "A photorealistic book cover illustration of a young asian woman with flowing black hair, wielding a staff that glows with blue light, casting a magical spell in a dense, moonlit forest with mist rising from the ground."

This revised prompt incorporates details about ethnicity, lighting, and atmosphere, resulting in a much more specific and visually compelling image.

Chapter 4: Shaping Your AI-Generated Vision: From Raw Output to Refined Design

The AI-generated image is your starting point. Now, let's refine it and integrate it into your design workflow:

- **Refining and Editing AI-Generated Images for Polish:**

    - Most generative AI tools offer editing tools within the platform. Use them to adjust lighting, colors, and minor details.

    - External image editing software like Photoshop can also be used for further refinement and compositing.

- **Combining AI-Generated Elements with Traditional Design Tools:**
  - Don't view AI-generated images as final products. Use them as a springboard for further design iterations.
  - Combine AI-generated elements with your own design skills using software like Adobe Illustrator to create a cohesive composition.
- **Building Moodboards and Design Systems with the Help of AI:**
  - Generate variations of a concept using the AI to explore different design directions and create mood boards for your project.

- Leverage AI-generated elements to build a consistent design system for your brand or project, ensuring visual coherence.

Imagine designing a website for a travel agency. You can use an AI tool to generate various images of exotic locations, then use those elements to build a cohesive website aesthetic.

By mastering the prompt and refining the outputs, you can harness the power of generative AI design to streamline your workflow and unlock a world of creative possibilities.

Part 3: AI Design Empowering Different Fields

Generative AI design is rapidly transforming various

creative industries. Let's explore how AI is

empowering designers in specific fields.

Chapter 5: Revolutionizing Graphic Design and

Illustration with AI

- **Generating Logos, Social Media Content, and**

  Marketing Materials:

- Struggling with logo ideas? Use AI to generate variations on a concept based on your brand keywords.

- Need fresh social media graphics? Prompt the AI to create eye-catching visuals for your next campaign.

- Save time brainstorming marketing materials. Let AI generate concepts for flyers, brochures, or presentations.

- **Creating Concept Art and Storyboards with AI Assistance:**

  - **Case Study: Concept Art for a Video Game** Imagine creating concept art for a fantasy video game. You can use prompts like "A fierce warrior princess riding a griffin over a medieval battlefield" to generate visuals that inspire your game's world and characters.

- Storyboarding Made Easier: Storyboards are crucial for planning films and animations. Use AI to generate quick sketches of scenes based on your descriptions, streamlining the storyboarding process.

Chapter 6: AI as a Catalyst in Product Design and Development

- **Exploring Design Variations and Brainstorming with AI:**

  - Stuck in a design rut? Generate multiple variations of a product concept using AI.

This "idea shower" can spark innovation and help you explore different possibilities.

- **Prototyping and User Interface (UI) Design with AI Tools:**

  - **Case Study: Prototyping a Mobile App** Designing a mobile app can be time-consuming. Use AI to generate basic layouts and mockups based on your wireframes. This allows you to quickly test functionalities and user interactions before investing significant design resources.

  - **UI Design Inspiration:** Need inspiration for your app's interface? Prompt the AI to generate various UI styles based on your

target audience and brand identity.

Chapter 7: The Future of Fashion and Architecture with AI Design

- **Generating New Design Trends and Exploring Possibilities:**

  - Fashion designers can use AI to generate unique textile patterns, clothing styles, and explore color combinations that push the boundaries of conventional design.

- **Creating Architectural Renderings and Floor Plans with AI:**
  - Architects can leverage AI to generate realistic 3D renderings of building designs, allowing clients to visualize the final structure before construction begins.
  - AI can also be used to create initial floor plans based on space requirements and functionality, saving architects time in the initial design phase.

By integrating AI design tools into their workflows, creatives across various fields can unlock new possibilities, expedite design processes, and ultimately bring their visions to life more efficiently.

Part 4: The Evolving Landscape of AI Design

As AI design continues to evolve, it's crucial to consider the ethical implications and how it will reshape the design landscape.

Advanced Techniques in Stable Diffusion: Design,

Customization, and Fine-Tuning

Stable Diffusion has rapidly emerged as a powerful

tool for generating high-quality images from textual

descriptions. It leverages cutting-edge deep learning models and diffusion techniques to produce images that are visually compelling and semantically accurate. Unlike other generative models, such as GANs (Generative Adversarial Networks), Stable Diffusion offers a highly flexible architecture that allows for fine-grained control over the generation process. This section delves into the advanced techniques for using Stable Diffusion in a design-centric context, focusing on customization, fine-tuning, and design principles that can elevate the quality and specificity of your generated images.

The core of Stable Diffusion lies in a denoising diffusion probabilistic model (DDPM). This architecture defines how an image is progressively generated through a series of noise steps, where the model learns to reverse the noise process to reconstruct the target image. Unlike traditional convolutional neural networks (CNNs), which perform direct pixel-to-pixel mapping, Stable Diffusion works through a latent space—an abstract representation of the image—allowing for more efficient generation and higher-quality outputs.

The model operates by introducing random noise into an image and then iteratively refining it to match the input prompt, such as a descriptive text. The model can be trained on millions of images and their corresponding text descriptions, enabling it to generate novel images based on a wide range of

textual inputs. However, to maximize the utility of

Stable Diffusion in real-world design workflows, one

must understand how to fine-tune the model to

produce results that are not only visually striking but

also closely aligned with specific creative goals.

Customizing Stable Diffusion for Specific Design Goals

One of the standout features of Stable Diffusion is its ability to be fine-tuned for specific design needs. This customization allows designers to better align the model's outputs with their vision, whether they are working in fashion, architecture, or entertainment. Fine-tuning involves retraining a pre-existing model on a domain-specific dataset. By doing so, the model can learn more about the specific characteristics of the target domain, producing more relevant and contextually appropriate images.

For example, if you're working on a project that requires futuristic architecture designs, fine-tuning

Stable Diffusion with a dataset of sci-fi buildings, cityscapes, or conceptual art can help the model learn the stylistic elements, color schemes, and design principles that define this genre. When you input a text prompt like "futuristic skyscraper with glass panels and neon lights," the model will generate outputs that are more likely to feature these characteristics, as opposed to a generic image generation.

Fine-tuning involves several steps, including selecting the right dataset, modifying the model architecture, and adjusting hyperparameters to ensure optimal performance. The training dataset is the foundation of the model's ability to generate context-specific content. In general, the more diverse and representative your dataset is of the desired domain, the better the results. Additionally, fine-tuning requires robust computational resources, as training large-scale diffusion models demands significant processing power.

Moreover, another customization method involves prompt engineering, which focuses on how text inputs are crafted to yield specific outputs. By carefully curating your prompts, you can guide the model to generate images that closely align with your creative vision. This practice can involve using highly descriptive language or adding context to the prompt to instruct the model on the desired level of abstraction, realism, or artistic style.

For instance, a designer working on fantasy art could input a prompt like "A magical forest with glowing trees and misty atmosphere, in the style of classic European fairy tale illustrations." The additional details on style and atmosphere direct the model to generate images that are faithful to the artistic traditions of that genre. In this way, Stable Diffusion's prompt engineering empowers designers to act as curators, shaping the AI's output to suit their particular aesthetic.

Hyperparameter Tuning for Enhanced Control

Once you have fine-tuned your Stable Diffusion model, controlling its behavior with hyperparameters is the next step to gaining precise control over the generated output. Hyperparameter tuning involves adjusting key settings that govern the model's operation during training and generation. These hyperparameters can drastically affect the quality, style, and relevance of the generated images.

Some important hyperparameters to consider in Stable Diffusion include:

- **Learning Rate:** The learning rate dictates how quickly the model adapts to new data during training. A higher learning rate can result in faster convergence but may also lead to instability, whereas a lower learning rate results in more gradual training but can improve model stability.

- **Noise Schedule:** The noise schedule defines how the noise is added and removed throughout the denoising process. Fine-tuning this schedule can impact the resolution and sharpness of the generated image. A more aggressive noise schedule might create more abstract or impressionistic results, while a smoother schedule can yield more detailed, realistic images.

- **Latent Space Dimensions:** The latent space is where the model encodes the image before transforming it into the final output. By adjusting the dimensions of this space, you can control how much information is retained during the diffusion process. Larger latent spaces capture more complex details, while smaller latent spaces may simplify the model but lose some nuance.

- **Guidance Scale:** The guidance scale is a key parameter in determining how strictly the model should follow the input text prompt. A higher guidance scale results in outputs that more closely match the prompt, while a lower scale allows for greater creativity and abstraction. Tuning the guidance scale is essential for generating images that balance fidelity to the prompt with the model's creative freedom.

By experimenting with these parameters and evaluating the results, you can refine the model's output to better suit your design needs. Achieving a balance between high-level control and creative freedom is one of the key challenges of working with generative AI models like Stable Diffusion. However, once mastered, this balance can result in highly customized, stunning visual outputs.

Leveraging Style Transfer and Post-Processing

Techniques

Another technique to enhance the results from Stable Diffusion is the use of style transfer, which allows you to apply specific artistic styles to your generated images. Style transfer is a technique borrowed from the realm of deep learning-based image manipulation, where the style of one image is applied to the content of another. This can be done by blending the aesthetic features of an artist's work, a particular design genre, or even the elements of multiple styles into the generated output.

For example, you might start with a basic image generated by Stable Diffusion based on a simple text prompt, such as "a serene mountain landscape." Then, by applying style transfer, you can manipulate the image to take on the look of an impressionistic painting or a photorealistic image. Tools like neural style transfer algorithms can be used in conjunction with Stable Diffusion to transform the output into something that reflects a particular visual identity or design trend.

Post-processing techniques also play a critical role in refining the final output. While Stable Diffusion is capable of generating impressive images on its own, further enhancement using tools like Adobe Photoshop or GIMP can make a significant difference. These tools allow designers to tweak the image's contrast, sharpness, color grading, and texture, as well as combine multiple outputs to create composite designs.

Additionally, it's possible to incorporate other AI-powered tools into your design pipeline. For example, using generative adversarial networks (GANs) for additional refinement or utilizing style transfer networks for specific artistic effects can further elevate the generated images. By integrating multiple AI techniques, you can expand the creative possibilities and develop a more diverse array of visual designs that are perfectly tailored to your needs.

Integrating Stable Diffusion into Design Pipelines

Integrating Stable Diffusion into a design pipeline allows you to automate and streamline the process of image creation. In a professional design environment, time is often a critical factor, and having an AI tool that can quickly generate creative ideas, mockups, or final designs can drastically improve productivity.

To effectively incorporate Stable Diffusion into a design workflow, it's crucial to consider the following components:

- **Data Management:** Organizing and storing the vast amount of data used to fine-tune and generate images is essential. Using cloud-based storage solutions or local data warehouses can make it easier to access and manage large datasets, allowing for smoother integration with Stable Diffusion.

- **API and Automation Tools:** Stable Diffusion offers API integration, which makes it easy to incorporate into web applications, mobile apps, or other design tools. Automating the image generation process through scripting or batch processing can speed up tasks like creating product mockups, generating marketing materials, or producing social media content.

- **Collaboration Tools:** For design teams, incorporating collaborative platforms that allow for sharing and feedback is crucial. By integrating Stable Diffusion with platforms like Slack, Trello, or Figma, teams can easily collaborate on visual designs, share generated content, and quickly iterate on ideas.

By creating a seamless flow of data, model generation, and output refinement, you can ensure that Stable Diffusion enhances rather than disrupts the design process. The result is a more agile, efficient, and creative workflow that empowers designers to produce high-quality, customized content in record time.

The Future of Stable Diffusion in Generative AI Design

Looking forward, the future of Stable Diffusion and other generative models in design is promising. As the technology continues to evolve, we can expect even greater advancements in model capabilities, fine-tuning precision, and integration with other AI tools. New architectures and optimization techniques will likely emerge, allowing for even more complex and realistic image generation.

Moreover, as generative AI models become more refined, they will become increasingly adept at capturing not just visual features but also abstract concepts, emotions, and narrative elements. Designers will be able to create images that evoke specific feelings or tell compelling stories, all generated through the power of AI. This capability will open up new opportunities for industries like advertising, film production, video game design, and more.

In summary, Stable Diffusion offers a wealth of possibilities for designers looking to explore the intersection of creativity and AI. By understanding the architecture, customization techniques, hyperparameter tuning, and integration strategies, you can unlock the full potential of this powerful tool. As generative AI continues to evolve, its role in the creative industries will only grow, offering exciting new avenues for artistic expression, design innovation, and business transformation.

Advanced Applications and Techniques in DALL-E 2 for Generative AI Design

DALL-E 2, the next iteration of OpenAI's revolutionary image generation model, takes the foundations laid by its predecessor and expands them into more robust, high-quality visual outputs. While Stable Diffusion focuses on high-level abstraction and control, DALL-E 2 offers a suite of additional tools that are particularly valuable for designers, including an innovative inpainting tool that allows users to edit and refine specific portions of generated images. This chapter explores advanced applications of DALL-E 2, showcasing how its unique features can be used to push the boundaries of creative design.

In comparison to Stable Diffusion, DALL-E 2 operates by transforming text prompts into images with extraordinary visual accuracy and coherence. The model is capable of understanding complex relationships between objects, materials, lighting conditions, and perspectives, making it particularly useful for industries that require precise and aesthetically pleasing results, such as product design, marketing, and entertainment.

Creative Control with DALL-E 2: Image Editing and Inpainting

One of the most exciting features of DALL-E 2 is its inpainting ability, which allows users to edit parts of an image while keeping the surrounding areas intact.

This functionality is incredibly powerful for designers who need to refine or tweak generated images for specific needs. For example, a designer might generate an image of a product prototype with a certain color scheme and then adjust the colors of a particular part of the design, or even replace a background to match the desired context.

Inpainting in DALL-E 2 works by first generating a base image based on the user's prompt. The user then selects the region of the image they wish to alter and provides new instructions for that portion. The model will intelligently update just the selected part of the image, seamlessly integrating it with the rest of the design. This technique is particularly useful for rapid prototyping, visual adjustments, and iterative design work, as it allows users to tweak images without starting from scratch.

To illustrate how this works in practice, consider the example of a product designer working on a line of furniture. Using a text prompt like "modern office chair with ergonomic features," DALL-E 2 might generate a complete image of the chair in a standard color and design. The designer might then use inpainting to change the fabric texture, the chair's color, or even the surroundings to fit a specific room setting, all while maintaining the initial image's consistency.

Additionally, prompt engineering can be combined with inpainting to guide the model toward specific creative goals. For instance, if a designer wants a chair that combines a vintage aesthetic with modern functionality, they might input a prompt like, "Vintage armchair with contemporary metal accents," and then use inpainting to adjust minor details such as the fabric pattern or shape. This combination of text-based input and inpainting gives the designer greater control over both the conceptual and visual aspects of the design.

Expanding Creative Possibilities: Beyond Text-to-Image

While DALL-E 2's text-to-image capabilities are groundbreaking, the model's true potential is realized when we begin to explore more unconventional use cases. DALL-E 2 can not only generate still images but can also be extended to create animated sequences, product variations, or even conceptual visualizations for marketing campaigns.

For instance, a designer working on a branding project could leverage DALL-E 2 to generate a series of variations of a logo, allowing them to quickly iterate on different visual concepts. By modifying the text prompts slightly, such as changing the colors or the overall style, the model can produce multiple, unique iterations of the same concept, saving valuable time and effort in the design process.

Moreover, DALL-E 2's ability to generate diverse visual content based on simple modifications opens up new possibilities for iterative design. Imagine designing a product line with variations on a theme, such as a series of fashion accessories. With DALL-E 2, the designer could generate variations of a scarf, hat, or watch by adjusting prompts like "golden watch with minimalist design" to create a broad array of designs,

helping to streamline the creative process.

Advanced Use Cases: From Concept to Completion

For designers, DALL-E 2 can be used throughout the creative process—from initial brainstorming and concept development to final design execution. This section explores how to integrate DALL-E 2 into the broader design pipeline, including how it can be used in advertising, branding, video production, and other creative fields.

In advertising, the speed at which creative assets need to be produced is a critical factor. DALL-E 2's ability to quickly generate high-quality images based on textual input allows marketing teams to test visual concepts, create mood boards, and develop ad creatives without relying on a lengthy design process. This can drastically reduce time-to-market for campaigns and give marketers a greater range of visual ideas to explore.

For example, a fashion brand looking to launch a new clothing line can use DALL-E 2 to generate a variety of potential campaign visuals that reflect different moods, settings, and concepts. A prompt like "luxurious high-fashion brand runway show" could be used to generate a set of images showcasing different runway scenes, lighting conditions, and models, giving the brand a pool of images to choose from.

Branding and Identity Design

Branding is another area where DALL-E 2 can be instrumental. Designers working on a logo or brand identity can input concepts related to the brand's core values and visual style. The model can then generate a range of logos and branding elements, such as business card designs, packaging concepts, and promotional materials. By experimenting with different textual prompts, designers can quickly create and refine a cohesive brand identity, all within

a matter of hours.

Challenges and Ethical Considerations in Using DALL-

E 2

As with any powerful tool, the use of generative AI

models like DALL-E 2 presents both opportunities and

challenges. While the model's ability to create high-quality images quickly is invaluable, it also raises ethical considerations regarding the authenticity of the generated content and the potential for misuse.

One of the most significant challenges with DALL-E 2 is ensuring that generated content respects the intellectual property and creative rights of original artists. Given the model's ability to generate art that closely resembles the work of human creators, there is the potential for copyright infringement or the unintentional reproduction of protected works. OpenAI has taken steps to mitigate this by implementing content moderation filters to prevent harmful or unethical content from being generated, but the responsibility also lies with users to be mindful of how they deploy the tool.

Another consideration is the potential for AI-generated content to perpetuate harmful stereotypes or biases. Since DALL-E 2 is trained on large datasets scraped from the internet, it may inadvertently reinforce societal biases present in the data. To address this, users should be vigilant about the inputs they provide and take steps to ensure that their generated content is inclusive and does not perpetuate discriminatory or harmful imagery.

As AI tools like DALL-E 2 continue to evolve, it is essential for designers to approach them with a critical eye, ensuring that they are used responsibly and ethically while harnessing their full creative

potential.

The Future of Generative AI in Design: Exploring New Frontiers

The future of generative AI tools like Stable Diffusion and DALL-E 2 is promising, as rapid advancements in the field are enabling more nuanced and creative applications. In the years to come, we can expect AI models to become even more powerful, with the ability to generate highly detailed and accurate images, integrate seamlessly with existing design tools, and offer even more customization options for users.

Future improvements may also lead to the integration of multimodal inputs, allowing users to combine not only text and images but also sounds, videos, and 3D models into the generative process. Such advancements would expand the capabilities of AI models, enabling designers to explore new realms of creativity and innovation in ways that were previously unimaginable.

Additionally, the increasing accessibility of generative AI tools will democratize the design process, allowing designers from all backgrounds and skill levels to leverage these powerful technologies. This shift will likely lead to an explosion of creativity, as people who may have lacked the resources or technical expertise to create high-quality visuals can now use AI to bring their ideas to life.

As these tools become more integrated into design workflows, the future of design will likely look very different, with AI playing a central role in shaping everything from product design to advertising, film production, and beyond.

By embracing the possibilities offered by generative AI, designers can push the boundaries of their craft, creating compelling and imaginative visuals that resonate with audiences in new and exciting ways.

Chapter 8: Navigating the Ethical Considerations of AI-Generated Design

- **Understanding Ownership and Copyright Issues in AI Design:**
    - Who owns the rights to an AI-generated image? The creator of the prompt, the developer of the AI tool, or is it a shared ownership? This is a complex legal question with ongoing debate.
- **Addressing Bias and Ensuring Fairness in AI-Generated Outputs:**
    - AI models are trained on massive datasets, and these datasets can contain inherent

biases. This can lead to AI-generated images that perpetuate stereotypes or lack diversity. Designers need to be aware of these biases and take steps to mitigate them when crafting prompts.

Case Study: Mitigating Bias in AI-Generated Marketing Materials

Imagine designing a marketing campaign for a fitness center. You want to ensure your AI-generated visuals represent a diverse range of body types and ethnicities. Here's how you can address bias:

* Include keywords like "body positive" and "diverse ethnicities" in your prompts.

* Provide the AI with reference images that showcase the desired inclusivity.

Case Study 1: Fashion Design Using Generative AI

Background:

A high-end fashion brand wanted to explore the potential of generative AI in designing new fashion lines. The company was looking for a tool that could generate creative yet relevant designs, helping the design team speed up the ideation process while ensuring that the generated designs met their brand's aesthetic and quality standards.

Application:

The brand chose to implement DALL-E 2 to generate a variety of fashion concepts based on text prompts. By providing prompts such as "luxurious red evening gown with intricate gold embroidery" or "futuristic metallic jacket with holographic effects," the AI was able to generate a diverse range of fashion designs that aligned with the brand's style.

The design team further refined the outputs using DALL-E 2's inpainting feature, allowing them to make specific adjustments to fabrics, colors, or patterns on certain parts of the generated images without starting from scratch. This helped streamline the process of prototyping, as they could quickly experiment with different styles and color combinations without manual drawing.

Outcome:

The use of generative AI significantly reduced the time it took to come up with new ideas and variations. The fashion designers were able to generate multiple

iterations in a single day, which would have taken

several weeks through traditional methods. This

increased the speed of decision-making, allowing the

brand to react to trends faster and release new

collections with greater agility.

Challenges and Insights:

One challenge faced was ensuring the generated

designs aligned with the brand's aesthetic and ethos.

To mitigate this, the team used carefully crafted

prompts and incorporated human oversight

throughout the process to guide the design choices.

Additionally, there was concern over the potential for

AI-generated designs to inadvertently replicate

existing trends, so the team used the outputs as inspiration rather than final products.

Case Study 2: Marketing and Advertising Campaigns

Background:

A global beverage company wanted to launch a new product in a highly competitive market. They needed creative assets for their advertising campaign, including digital ads, social media posts, and website banners. The challenge was to generate visually striking content quickly and cost-effectively.

Application:

The marketing team used DALL-E 2 to generate a wide

variety of creative assets based on prompts such as "vibrant tropical fruit drink with ice and fresh herbs" or "refreshing lemonade in a summer beach setting." DALL-E 2's ability to generate images in different styles allowed them to experiment with everything from hyper-realistic photos to artistic illustrations that reflected different aspects of the brand's identity.

Once initial concepts were generated, the team used DALL-E 2's inpainting feature to fine-tune specific elements, such as adjusting the drink's color or replacing the background with an image of a beach or urban landscape. The team also used the AI model to create different variations of the visuals, enabling them to A/B test which images performed best in terms of audience engagement.

Outcome:

The use of DALL-E 2 accelerated the asset creation process, reducing the time required to produce high-quality visuals from weeks to just a few days. The team was able to generate multiple variations and select the best-performing ones for the campaign. This led to higher engagement rates on digital platforms, as the visuals resonated with consumers in different regions and demographics.

Challenges and Insights:

One challenge encountered was ensuring that the generated images aligned with brand guidelines, as the AI sometimes produced outputs that were too abstract or diverged from the desired visual style. By providing detailed and specific prompts and curating the results carefully, the team was able to address these issues.

Case Study 3: Real Estate Virtual Staging

Background:

A real estate agency faced difficulty showcasing vacant properties to potential buyers. Traditional virtual staging was expensive and time-consuming, so the agency sought a more efficient and cost-effective solution to create visually appealing property images.

Application:

The agency turned to Stable Diffusion to create realistic, digitally staged interiors of the homes they were selling. By providing text prompts such as "modern living room with white walls and contemporary furniture" or "spacious kitchen with marble countertops and stainless steel appliances," they were able to generate images that accurately reflected the potential of the space.

Stable Diffusion allowed the team to experiment with different styles of furniture, color schemes, and layouts without physically rearranging or buying new items. This gave them a range of visual options that could be tailored to different buyer demographics, from minimalist design to more traditional or luxurious interiors.

Outcome:

Generative AI greatly reduced the cost and time associated with traditional virtual staging. The agency could now create multiple staged images for each property, showcasing different potential uses of the space. This enhanced the property listings and led to faster sales and higher engagement from prospective buyers.

Challenges and Insights:

One challenge was ensuring that the generated images did not look too artificial or unnatural. The team had to carefully craft prompts and occasionally combine AI-generated images with real photographs

to achieve the right balance of realism and visual

appeal.

Case Study 4: Concept Art for Video Games

Background:

A video game studio was working on a new game and

needed concept art for various in-game environments,

characters, and assets. The challenge was that the studio had a small art team and tight deadlines, meaning they needed to find ways to generate a large volume of concept art quickly.

Application:

The studio used DALL-E 2 to generate initial concept art for characters, weapons, and environments based on detailed text prompts. For example, a prompt like "futuristic cityscape with neon lights and towering skyscrapers" or "ancient temple with stone carvings and moss-covered walls" resulted in striking visual concepts that the team could refine.

Once the initial images were generated, the team used the inpainting feature to modify elements of the designs, such as changing the color palette of a character's armor or adding additional details to an environment. This allowed them to iterate on ideas quickly and present the designs to stakeholders for approval faster than they could with traditional methods.

Outcome:

Generative AI helped the studio produce a wide range of concept art in a fraction of the time it would have taken with traditional methods. This not only saved time but also inspired new creative ideas that the team had not considered before. The ability to generate multiple design variations allowed them to explore different aesthetics and thematic elements for the game.

Challenges and Insights:

The main challenge was maintaining consistency in style and design across different concepts. The team overcame this by refining their prompts to ensure a consistent visual language and regularly iterating on the results to align with the game's narrative and art direction.

Case Study 5: Product Design for Prototypes

Background:

An industrial design company specializing in consumer electronics wanted to explore new product concepts without committing significant resources to the early stages of design. The goal was to generate visual prototypes quickly, assess their feasibility, and iterate on ideas before moving to physical models.

Application:

The design team used Stable Diffusion to generate various product concepts based on prompts such as "sleek smartphone with curved edges" or "minimalist smart speaker with integrated touch controls." By providing detailed text descriptions, they were able to generate highly detailed product prototypes that included textures, materials, and functional components.

Using Stable Diffusion's high-level abstraction, they could experiment with different design directions before committing to a physical prototype. The ability to generate 3D mockups and conceptual designs allowed them to test out a broad array of design ideas quickly.

Outcome:

Generative AI allowed the team to produce visual prototypes in a fraction of the time it would have taken using traditional CAD software. This helped reduce costs and speed up the decision-making process, allowing the design team to explore more ideas and present them to clients more effectively.

Challenges and Insights:

One challenge was that AI-generated designs sometimes lacked the level of detail or technical feasibility needed for real-world production. The team addressed this by using the AI-generated images as a conceptual tool, which was then translated into more refined designs using CAD software.

Chapter 9: The Human-AI Design Partnership: A New Era of Collaboration

- **How AI is Transforming the Role of Designers:**
  - AI is not replacing designers, but rather augmenting their capabilities. Designers will need to develop new skills in crafting prompts, understanding AI limitations, and integrating AI-generated elements into their workflow.

- **New Design Workflows and Processes Emerging with AI:**
  - Traditional design processes will be streamlined. AI can handle repetitive tasks like generating variations and initial

concepts, freeing designers to focus on the strategic and creative aspects of design.

Case Study: A Collaborative Design Workflow with AI

A graphic designer working on a website can use AI to generate various color palettes and layout options. They can then use these AI outputs as a starting point, refine them in design software, and incorporate their own design flourishes to create a unique final product.

Chapter 10: A Glimpse Ahead: What the Future Holds for AI Design

- **Exploring AI-Powered Design Automation:**

  - In the future, AI might be able to handle entire design projects with minimal human intervention. This could raise questions about the value of human creativity in the design field.

- **Democratizing Design with User-Friendly AI Tools:**

  - AI design tools are becoming increasingly user-friendly. This opens the door for non-designers to create basic visuals, potentially democratizing design and

making it more accessible to everyone.

Conclusion: The Limitless Potential of Generative AI Design

Generative AI design is a powerful tool with the potential to revolutionize how we create visual content across various fields. By understanding its capabilities, limitations, and ethical considerations, designers can leverage AI to enhance their workflows, explore new creative possibilities, and ultimately

shape the future of design.

Chapter : Generative AI in Healthcare and Medical Research

Background: The healthcare industry has long relied on traditional methods for drug discovery, diagnostics, and medical imaging. However, the complexity and time-consuming nature of these processes led to an interest in leveraging new technologies to accelerate breakthroughs. The rise of generative AI, particularly models like DALL-E 2 and Stable Diffusion, has opened new avenues in healthcare, from creating synthetic data to enhancing diagnostic tools.

Application: In the field of medical imaging, Stable Diffusion has been used to generate high-quality synthetic images for training AI models. For example, a research team used generative AI to generate realistic CT scans and MRI images of organs and tissues, allowing them to create a larger dataset for training deep learning algorithms that can assist doctors in diagnosing conditions like tumors or fractures. By training AI models on these synthetic datasets, the research team was able to improve the accuracy and efficiency of diagnostic models.

Similarly, DALL-E 2 has been used to generate conceptual visualizations of new medical devices or drug delivery systems. Prompts like "3D rendering of a drug delivery system for targeted cancer treatment" or "futuristic MRI machine design with integrated AI" have produced valuable design concepts that serve as the basis for engineering teams to explore. These designs can streamline the prototyping phase, reducing time and cost.

Outcome: The ability to generate synthetic medical images has provided an essential tool for researchers and clinicians working with limited datasets. Generative AI has also helped in designing innovative medical devices and systems, ultimately speeding up the development of next-generation healthcare technologies. In particular, these tools have helped bridge gaps in training AI systems, reducing reliance on real-world datasets that can be expensive and difficult to obtain.

Challenges and Insights: A key challenge in using generative AI in healthcare is ensuring that the AI-generated images and designs meet clinical standards. While these models can generate highly realistic outputs, they need careful validation to ensure their accuracy in real-world scenarios. Moreover, privacy and ethical concerns are at the forefront of healthcare AI. Generating synthetic patient data must be done in a way that respects patient privacy and complies with healthcare regulations.

Chapter : Generative AI in Video Production and

Animation

Background: The video production industry has undergone a dramatic transformation with the advent of new AI-driven tools. Traditionally, video production involved a labor-intensive process, requiring significant time and resources to create everything from special effects to animations. However, generative AI models like Stable Diffusion and DALL-E 2 have revolutionized this process by enabling the creation of high-quality visual content in a fraction of the time.

Application: Generative AI is increasingly being used to create concept art, visual effects, and even entire scenes for video productions. For example, in a recent animation project, a production team used DALL-E 2 to generate background art based on text prompts such as "a post-apocalyptic city with crumbling buildings and dark skies" or "a lush, enchanted forest with glowing plants and mystical creatures." The ability to quickly generate visually striking and consistent backgrounds allowed the team to focus on the character animations and storyline rather than spending weeks designing and rendering the environment.

In the realm of video effects, Stable Diffusion has been used to generate photorealistic elements like fire, explosions, and smoke. By providing specific prompts such as "realistic explosion in an urban setting" or "smoke billowing from a burning building," the team was able to integrate AI-generated elements into live-action footage seamlessly, saving time and reducing costs associated with traditional CGI techniques.

Outcome: Generative AI has significantly reduced the time required to produce high-quality visuals for film and television. By generating backgrounds, special effects, and other visual assets quickly, video production teams can experiment with different looks and styles without committing significant resources to each shot. This has allowed smaller studios and independent creators to compete with larger studios, as the barrier to entry for high-quality production has lowered.

Challenges and Insights: One of the main challenges in using generative AI for video production is maintaining consistency across shots, especially in long-form content. While DALL-E 2 and Stable Diffusion can generate stunning visuals, ensuring that the AI-generated elements align with the overall tone and style of the video can be difficult. Production teams have to carefully curate and refine the outputs to ensure consistency across multiple scenes or episodes.

Chapter : Generative AI in Architecture and Urban Planning

Background: Architecture and urban planning are fields that rely heavily on visualization and conceptual design. Architects and urban planners have traditionally used CAD software and manual sketching to bring their ideas to life. However, the advent of generative AI has provided a new way to create and refine architectural designs, making it easier for professionals to visualize their concepts in a more dynamic and efficient way.

Application: In architecture, Stable Diffusion has been used to generate design variations for buildings, landscapes, and urban spaces. By providing detailed text prompts such as "futuristic skyscraper with a glass façade and green rooftop" or "open-concept office with minimalist design and large windows," architects can quickly generate multiple iterations of a building or interior design. These AI-generated designs can serve as the foundation for further refinement, saving time in the early conceptual stages.

Urban planners have also utilized DALL-E 2 to visualize entire cityscapes. By generating concepts for transportation systems, green spaces, and commercial areas, planners can quickly assess how their designs would look in the real world. For example, a city's redesign might involve generating images of "a pedestrian-friendly street lined with trees and benches" or "a public park with water features and open spaces." These images help planners communicate their ideas to stakeholders and the public more effectively.

Outcome: Generative AI has allowed architects and urban planners to create more diverse and innovative designs in less time. The ability to generate multiple iterations of a design quickly has led to more experimentation and creative thinking. Additionally, AI-generated visualizations have helped improve communication with clients and stakeholders, as they provide a clearer and more tangible representation of a concept than sketches or written descriptions.

Challenges and Insights: One challenge faced by architects and urban planners is ensuring that AI-generated designs meet the technical and regulatory standards required for real-world construction. While AI can generate aesthetically pleasing designs, these outputs often need to be refined and adjusted to meet safety codes, environmental standards, and client requirements. Moreover, as with other industries, there is the issue of bias in AI-generated designs. AI models may unintentionally favor certain architectural styles or features, limiting diversity in design solutions.

Chapter : Leveraging Generative AI for Product

Design and Prototyping

Generative AI and Its Role in Product Design

The process of product design traditionally involves a series of iterative steps: concept creation, prototyping, user testing, refinement, and final manufacturing. The creative and technical aspects of product design require collaboration between designers, engineers, and stakeholders to align aesthetics with functionality. However, the integration of generative AI into the product design lifecycle has accelerated this process significantly, enabling designers to explore a wider range of design possibilities without the need for extensive manual input or resources.

Generative AI models, such as DALL-E 2 and Stable Diffusion, have been increasingly used in various industries for rapid product ideation, design conceptualization, and prototyping. By using simple text prompts, designers can now generate multiple iterations of a product concept, each exploring different styles, materials, forms, and functionalities. These AI models can produce detailed, realistic visual representations, which help designers assess the viability of ideas in a fraction of the time.

AI-Driven Ideation and Conceptualization

One of the key advantages of generative AI in product design is its ability to generate a large number of diverse design concepts quickly. A designer working on a new smartphone, for example, can provide prompts such as "sleek, ultra-thin smartphone design with curved edges and holographic display" or "rugged, heavy-duty phone with interchangeable modular components." In just a few moments, Stable Diffusion can produce a wide variety of design outputs, helping the designer visualize multiple possibilities.

This ability to rapidly generate new concepts helps eliminate the lengthy brainstorming and sketching stages traditionally associated with product design. The designs produced by DALL-E 2 or Stable Diffusion can also be used as starting points for more refined, CAD-based modeling. Additionally, AI-generated designs are not constrained by the limitations of traditional design tools, allowing for innovative solutions that may not have been considered through conventional methods.

Prototyping with Generative AI

Once an initial product design concept has been generated, the next phase in product development is prototyping. Traditionally, this phase requires significant investment in materials, machinery, and labor. However, generative AI, paired with 3D printing and additive manufacturing, has introduced a more efficient and cost-effective way to prototype products.

By using DALL-E 2 or Stable Diffusion to generate 3D models or renderings of product components, designers can quickly assess the form, structure, and functionality of a design. These AI-generated prototypes can be exported into CAD software or 3D modeling programs, where engineers can prepare them for physical fabrication. With 3D printing, the physical models can be created quickly, allowing for hands-on testing and iteration, reducing the need for costly revisions during the development process.

Generative AI also enables the creation of optimized designs that are more efficient in terms of material usage. For example, AI can help generate products that minimize waste or use more sustainable materials, which can be crucial for industries with a focus on sustainability. The AI model can be prompted with specific constraints, such as "design a lightweight, ergonomic tool made of biodegradable plastic," to generate prototypes that meet environmental standards.

Outcome and Future Prospects

The integration of generative AI into product design and prototyping has not only reduced the time and cost involved but has also unlocked a new era of creativity. Designers now have the capability to explore ideas that were previously unimaginable due to resource limitations or technical constraints. AI-generated designs are enabling faster go-to-market timelines, more innovative products, and enhanced collaboration between designers, engineers, and manufacturers.

As AI continues to evolve, it will likely play an even more significant role in product lifecycle management. From fully autonomous product generation to AI-driven product testing and feedback loops, the future of product design is set to be even more dynamic and responsive to user needs.

Challenges and Ethical Considerations

Despite the benefits, generative AI in product design faces its challenges. One issue is ensuring that the designs meet safety and regulatory standards. While AI can generate innovative ideas, human oversight is crucial to ensure that products are functional, manufacturable, and safe to use. Another consideration is the ethical use of AI-generated designs, particularly in cases where designs may unintentionally infringe on existing patents or intellectual property rights. Companies must ensure that AI-generated products do not inadvertently duplicate or steal from existing designs.

Chapter : Generative AI in Fashion and Apparel Design

Revolutionizing Fashion Design with AI

Fashion is an ever-evolving industry, and the pressure to stay ahead of trends while maintaining originality can be overwhelming. Traditionally, fashion design has been an artisanal process that relies heavily on creativity, intuition, and a deep understanding of materials and aesthetics. However, generative AI tools like DALL-E 2 and Stable Diffusion are beginning to reshape this process, bringing efficiency, scalability, and enhanced creativity to designers worldwide.

Generative AI models can be used to create fashion collections, predict upcoming trends, and generate entirely new designs that are visually appealing and innovative. By providing AI with textual prompts such as "vintage-inspired floral dress with asymmetrical cut" or "futuristic suit with metallic accents," designers can receive multiple design iterations that explore various color palettes, materials, and silhouettes. These AI-driven tools also allow designers to visualize how different fabrics and patterns will look together before committing to the production process.

Designing Fashion with Generative AI

The fashion design process is highly dependent on the visual appeal of the final product, and generative AI has been particularly valuable in this area. DALL-E 2, for example, can generate high-resolution images of clothing designs based on detailed text descriptions. Designers can experiment with different styles, textures, and patterns by simply modifying their prompts. A fashion designer might input prompts such as "high-fashion winter coat with faux fur collar" or "sporty chic jumpsuit with neon accents," and the model will produce various interpretations of these ideas, each offering a different take on the initial concept.

Additionally, AI tools allow designers to simulate how a design might look when worn by a human body. By generating realistic fashion renderings of clothing on digital models, designers can quickly evaluate the visual impact of their creations without needing to create physical samples. This capability not only saves time but also minimizes the environmental impact of sample production, which traditionally requires physical materials and resources.

Customization and Personalization

Another major benefit of generative AI in fashion is its ability to enable mass customization and personalized designs. With AI models, designers can offer customers personalized products that are tailored to individual tastes and preferences. A user could input specific requests, such as "design a dress with a floral pattern in pastel colors" or "create a custom jacket with a leather finish and gold accents," and the AI model would generate a design based on those preferences.

Brands are already beginning to incorporate AI-generated fashion into their offerings. Companies that specialize in custom apparel, such as bespoke tailoring or personalized fashion lines, can leverage AI to enhance the customer experience and deliver highly individualized products. By enabling customers to participate in the design process through simple text descriptions, AI opens up new opportunities for co-creation and creative expression in fashion.

Outcome and Market Impact

Generative AI in fashion offers numerous benefits to both designers and consumers. For designers, AI tools help generate new ideas quickly, streamline the design process, and eliminate the labor-intensive aspects of fashion creation. Consumers benefit from greater access to personalized clothing and unique designs that match their specific preferences.

The ability to rapidly generate new designs also provides fashion brands with a competitive edge. By incorporating generative AI into their design process, brands can stay ahead of trends and create new collections at a faster pace. Furthermore, AI allows brands to test new styles and concepts in the market without committing to costly production runs, minimizing risk and ensuring that only popular designs are brought to life.

Challenges and Ethical Considerations

Despite the opportunities, the use of generative AI in fashion is not without challenges. One key issue is the potential for homogenization. While AI can generate unique designs, there is a risk that the outputs may start to reflect trends that are already popular, rather than pushing the boundaries of creativity. Fashion is an art form, and some critics argue that AI-generated designs may lack the emotional depth and originality that human designers bring to the table.

Additionally, there are concerns about the ethical implications of using AI in fashion, particularly regarding intellectual property. AI models trained on vast amounts of data may inadvertently replicate elements of existing designs, potentially leading to

copyright disputes. Designers and brands will need to

ensure that AI-generated designs are original and

respect the intellectual property rights of others.

Future Trends in Generative AI Design:

The world of generative AI design is rapidly evolving, and the future holds exciting possibilities for how we create and interact with visual content. Here are some key trends to watch out for in the coming years:

1. Enhanced Creativity and Control:

- We can expect AI models to become more adept at understanding complex prompts and generating outputs that not only adhere to the descriptions but also exhibit a level of creativity that rivals human designers.

- Advancements in text-to-image translation will allow for more nuanced control over the style, mood, and composition of the generated images. Imagine prompting the AI to create a painting in the style of Van Gogh but with a futuristic setting.

2. Multimodal Design with AI:

- The future lies in the integration of generative AI with other design tools. We'll see AI collaborating with 3D modeling software to create realistic product renderings or working alongside animation tools to generate dynamic video content.

- This multimodal approach will empower designers to create immersive and interactive experiences that transcend static images.

3. AI-Powered Design Assistants:

- Generative AI tools are evolving from standalone applications to intelligent design assistants. These AI assistants will anticipate designers' needs, suggest relevant prompts and reference materials, and even provide feedback on generated outputs.

- Imagine an AI assistant that analyzes your brand identity and suggests design concepts that perfectly align with your brand aesthetic.

4. Democratization of Design with User-Friendly AI:

- As AI design tools become more user-friendly and intuitive, the barrier to entry for design creation will significantly decrease. We'll see the emergence of user-friendly interfaces that allow anyone, regardless of technical expertise, to generate basic visuals for presentations, social media posts, or even simple marketing materials.

- This democratization of design has the potential to empower individuals and small businesses to create professional-looking visuals without relying on professional designers.

5. Personalization and Customization Through AI:

- Generative AI will play a significant role in personalizing the design experience. Imagine AI tools that can generate design elements based on your individual preferences, color palettes inspired by your favorite artwork, or even layouts that adapt to the specific needs of your target audience.

- This level of personalization will create a more engaging and tailored design experience for users.

6. Ethical Considerations and Transparency:

- As AI design becomes more sophisticated, ethical considerations like bias in AI outputs and ownership of AI-generated content will need to be addressed.

- We'll see a growing focus on developing transparent AI design tools that users can understand and trust. Additionally, discussions around copyright and ownership of AI-generated creations will likely continue to evolve.

7. Explainable AI for Design Decisions:

- A crucial aspect of building trust in AI design tools is explainability. In the future, AI models might be able to explain their design decisions, allowing designers to understand why a particular image was generated and how the AI interpreted the prompt.

8. Generative AI for Design Education:

- Generative AI tools can be valuable assets in design education. Students can use AI to experiment with different design concepts, explore various styles, and rapidly prototype their ideas.

- This can foster a more iterative and exploratory learning experience for design students.

9. Generative AI in Unexpected Fields:

- The impact of generative AI design will extend beyond traditional design fields. We can expect to see AI-generated content used in scientific research, urban planning, and even product development.

- For example, AI might be used to generate initial prototypes for new inventions or create simulations of urban environments for better planning purposes.

10. The Human-AI Design Symbiosis:

- The future of design lies not in AI replacing humans, but in a collaborative partnership between the two. AI will handle time-consuming and repetitive tasks, freeing up designers to focus on the strategic and creative aspects of design.

- This human-AI collaboration will lead to a new era of design innovation and push the boundaries of what's possible in the visual realm.

The future of generative AI design is brimming with possibilities. As AI tools continue to evolve and become more sophisticated, we can expect a significant transformation in how we create, interact with, and experience visual content across various aspects of our lives.